BARRON'S BOOK NOTES

HENRY DAVID THOREAU'S
Walden

BY

Linda Corrente

SERIES EDITOR

Michael Spring
Editor, *Literary Cavalcade*
Scholastic Inc.

BARRON'S EDUCATIONAL SERIES, INC.
Woodbury, New York / London / Toronto / Sydney

ACKNOWLEDGMENTS

We would like to acknowledge the many painstaking hours of work Holly Hughes and Thomas F. Hirsch have devoted to making the *Book Notes* series a success.

All inquiries should be addressed to:
Barron's Educational Series, Inc.
113 Crossways Park Drive
Woodbury, New York 11797

Library of Congress Catalog Card No. 84-18528

International Standard Book No. 0-7641-9130-6

Library of Congress Cataloging in Publication Data
Corrente, Linda.
    Henry David Thoreau's Walden.

    (Barron's book notes)
    Bibliography: p. 78
    Summary: A guide to reading "Walden" with a critical and appreciative mind. Includes background on the author's life and times, sample tests, term paper suggestions, and a reading list.
        1. Thoreau, Henry David, 1817–1862. Walden.
    [1. Thoreau, Henry David, 1817–1862. Walden. 2. American Literature—History and criticism] I. Title. II. Series.
    PS3048.C67 1984   818.303   84-18528
    ISBN 0-7641-9130-6

PRINTED IN THE UNITED STATES OF AMERICA

456   550   98765432

CONTENTS

ADVISORY BOARD

HOW TO USE THIS BOOK

You have to know how to approach literature in order to get the most out of it. This *Barron's Book Notes* volume follows a plan based on methods used by some of the best students to read a work of literature.

Begin with the guide's section on the author's life and times. As you read, try to form a clear picture of the author's personality, circumstances, and motives for writing the work. This background usually will make it easier for you to hear the author's tone of voice, and follow where the author is heading.

Then go over the rest of the introductory material—such sections as those on the plot, characters, setting, themes, and style of the work. Underline, or write down in your notebook, particular things to watch for, such as contrasts between characters and repeated literary devices. At this point, you may want to develop a system of symbols to use in marking your text as you read. (Of course, you should only mark up a book you own, not one that belongs to another person or a school.) Perhaps you will want to use a different letter for each character's name, a different number for each major theme of the book, a different color for each important symbol or literary device. Be prepared to mark up the pages of your book as you read. Put your marks in the margins so you can find them again easily.

Now comes the moment you've been waiting for—the time to start reading the work of literature. You may want to put aside your *Barron's Book Notes* volume until you've read the work all the way through. Or you may want to alternate, reading the *Book Notes* analysis of each section as soon as you have finished reading the corresponding part of the original. Before you move on, reread crucial passages you don't fully understand. (Don't take this guide's analysis for granted—make up your own mind as to what the work means.)

Once you've finished the whole work of literature, you may want to review it right away, so you can firm up your ideas about what it means. You may want to leaf through the book concentrating on passages you marked in reference to one character or one theme. This is also a good time to reread the *Book Notes* introductory material, which pulls together insights on specific topics.

When it comes time to prepare for a test or to write a paper, you'll already have formed ideas about the work. You'll be able to go back through it, refreshing your memory as to the author's exact words and perspective, so that you can support your opinions with evidence drawn straight from the work. Patterns will emerge, and ideas will fall into place; your essay question or term paper will almost write itself. Give yourself a dry run with one of the sample tests in the guide. These tests present both multiple-choice and essay questions. An accompanying section gives answers to the multiple-choice questions as well as suggestions for writing the essays. If you have to select a term paper topic, you may choose one from the list of suggestions in this book. This guide also provides you with a reading list, to help you when you start research for a term paper, and a selection of provocative comments by critics, to spark your thinking before you write.

THE AUTHOR AND HIS TIMES

> Moreover, I, on my side, require of every writer, first or last, a simple and sincere account of his own life, and not merely what he has heard of other men's lives; some such account as he would send to his kindred from a distant land; for if he has lived sincerely it must have been in a distant land to me.

What sort of man might go off for two years to live alone in a cabin in the woods—to hoe beans, observe nature, and write in his journal? A deeply religious person, perhaps, one anxious for solitude. Or a person who wanted to escape a nine-to-five routine.

For years Henry David Thoreau talked about living alone in a cabin in the woods. He finally went to live at Walden Pond in 1845 when he was almost twenty-eight years old. In those days, most twenty-eight-year-old men were well into their careers. Not only did Henry not have a career, he didn't want one. After working only a few weeks, he had resigned from his job as a teacher in the Concord school system because he refused to beat his students into good behavior. With his older brother John, he then started his own school. It was quite a success until John's health failed and Henry was unable to keep the school open on his own.

Henry spent some time in his family's business of pencil making. He worked for a while as a surveyor. He also worked as a handyman and gardener for the family of Ralph Waldo Emerson, the philosopher and writer. In spite of all these jobs, he simply didn't have the same ambitions as other men.

Events in his personal life were so unsatisfying that Thoreau had nothing to lose in going off alone. One summer he fell in love with a young woman from Boston named Ellen Sewall; so did his brother John. John proposed to her, but she changed her mind and rejected him. Not knowing that his brother had proposed and been turned down, Henry proposed to her himself the next fall. By this time Ellen's father had developed an unfavorable opinion of the Thoreau family. He was convinced that they were too liberal for his liking, and he would not allow Ellen to marry Henry.

A year and a half later, Henry suffered a much greater loss: the death of his brother. John cut himself one day while sharpening a razor. He developed tetanus (at that time more commonly called "lockjaw") and ten days later he was dead.

From our position in the late twentieth century, surrounded as we are by synthetics and machines, it's easy to understand a person's desire to "get back to nature." A return to things that are natural, especially foods and fabrics, is fashionable today. But you may wonder why someone felt it necessary to live this way almost 150 years ago, when life was simpler, and people lived in closer harmony with nature.

The railroad had just come to Concord when Thoreau went to live at Walden. In Thoreau's world, the railroad was a symbol of commerce and of the Industrial Revolution. With the growth of industry came factory work with its poor conditions, low pay, and division of labor (each person doing only part of a job). Paralleling the rise of industry was a philosophy of materialism this country had not seen before. The Civil War had not yet been fought and slavery in the United States was still permitted. When Thoreau moved to Walden Pond he was reacting both against the problems and to the issues of his times.

Among the controversial issues of his time was the Transcendentalist movement. Ralph Waldo Emerson, with whom Thoreau lived and worked, had since the 1820s been a mouthpiece of the movement along with Thoreau's other Concord neighbors, Orestes Brownson and Bronson Alcott. (Thoreau was one of their disciples.)

In its beginnings Transcendentalism was a religious protest. Young clergymen in the Boston area were speaking out against the Unitarian Church. They objected to the Unitarian's view of man, which was influenced by John Locke who believed that man is born a blank slate and receives impressions through his senses. Through his senses, according to Locke, a man gathers *evidence* of the supernatural and the divine, but he can never experience or *know* God firsthand.

Transcendentalists believed that man was not a passive and limited being; he could imagine God. Since *imagining* something is in a way *creating* something, man could *create* God. And to take it one step further, any being who was capable of creating the divine must be divine himself. The movement was also characterized by an interest in Asian literature and mysticism. Followers believed they were responsible for spreading the truths they had gained. The Transcendentalists were convinced, too, that the way to attain spiritual growth was through nature.

By 1845 Henry was anxious to write his book-length account of a trip he had taken in a homemade rowboat years earlier with his brother John. It would become his first published work, *A Week on the Concord and Merrimack Rivers*. But, like every young artist, he was struggling to make time for his art while having to earn a living. When he figured out the cost of something, Henry always looked past the price expressed in dollars. He counted also the amount of time (spent working to earn those dollars) that he had to exchange in order to have the item. His solution to the problem was not to earn more, but to need less—to see if he might make himself richer by making his wants fewer. By Henry's standards, "Man is rich in proportion to the things that he can afford to let alone."

Emerson owned property at Walden Pond, a place between Concord and Lincoln, Massachusetts. Henry had loved this property since he was a boy. Emerson offered to let him build a cabin on its shore. Henry accepted, and lived there from March 1845 to September 1847. *Walden* is the record of his "experiment in living."

After Walden, Henry went first to live at the Emerson house, and later back to live with his father. He returned to his odd jobs and pencil making, adding some lecturing to his schedule. He continued to write in his journal, and to walk in the woods for some part of every day. He never married.

Thoreau died of tuberculosis in 1862 at the age of forty-four. His gravestone bears the single word *Henry*, and stands near the gravestones of Louisa May Alcott, Ralph Waldo Emerson, and Nathaniel Hawthorne on Author's Ridge in Sleepy Hollow Cemetery in Concord. All his life he refused to attend church. He considered the Bible a good book, but no more important than many others. On his deathbed Henry was asked if he had "made his peace" with God. God and he—the answer came—had never quarreled.

THE BOOK

Synopsis

In the mid 1800s a man named Henry David Thoreau borrowed an axe and built himself a cabin on the shore of Walden Pond in the woods near Boston. He then lived there, alone, for a little more than two years. He did as little work as possible, only what was absolutely necessary. He wanted to get away from what he called "the lives of quiet desperation" that most men led. He wanted to see if he could become "rich" by making his wants few. He raised beans, observed nature, and wrote in his journal. Seven years after he left the cabin *Walden: or, Life in the Woods* was published.

Walden may appear to be only a series of essays on topics that don't seem to have much in common—topics such as "Reading" and "The Bean-Field"—but it does follow a literary plan. In the first few chapters Thoreau defines what he called his "experiment in living." He describes *how* he lived the way he did, how he fed and clothed and housed himself. He also describes *why* he lived the way he did: "I went to the woods because I wished to live deliberately, to front only the essential facts of life, and see if I could not learn what it had to teach, and not, when I came to die, discover that I had not lived."

In order to "learn what it [life] had to teach" Thoreau follows many courses. He studies what can be read in the language of literature, and what can be heard in the language of nature. He studies what it means to be solitary. He studies with visitors what it is to be in the company of others.

You follow him through the book—along his travel through space and time—through space first, as he takes you with him, wandering away from his cabin to explore neighboring ponds, the village, and a farm. Then you follow through time as you watch the seasons unfurl in his life: first spring and the building of the cabin; then summer and fall on his walks; then winter with its own society; and then spring again, and the renewal he is always seeking.

When he decides it is time for him to leave the cabin on Walden Pond, he tells you this reason as clearly as he told you his reasons for going: "I left the woods for as good a reason as I went there. Perhaps it seemed to me that I had several more lives to live, and could not spare any more time for that one."

Thoreau answered the question about whether he had learned what the experiment had to teach, by saying:

> I learned this, at least, by my experiment: that if one advances confidently in the direction of his dreams, and endeavors to live the life which he has imagined, he will meet with a success unexpected in common hours. . . . If you have built castles in the air, your work need not be lost; that is where they should be. Now put the foundations under them.

Other Elements

SETTING

There is scarcely a page of *Walden* that does not make some reference to the place in which it is set. The pond is located in the Massachusetts woods between the towns of Concord and Lincoln, near Boston. Walden is a small pond, a half-mile long and a mile and three quarters around. Its shore is paved with rounded white stones, except for a couple of small sandy beaches. The water is clear and its color depends on the place from which it is viewed. Wooded hills rise up around it on all sides so that it is impossible to see anything beyond it. It has some fish, and it is populated by an assortment of animals and waterfowl.

The cabin that Thoreau built there was shingled and plastered, ten by fifteen feet. It had a chimney with a brick fireplace at one end, a door at the other, and one large window on each side.

Setting refers not only to the site in which a work takes place, it refers to the time in which it takes place, as well. *Walden* is set during a two-year period between 1845 and 1847 when Henry Thoreau lived at Walden Pond. It was a time before the Civil War, when slavery was still permitted. It was also a time when the Industrial Revolution was taking place, bringing division of labor, factories with poor working conditions and low pay, and a new breed of materialism. And it was the time of the Transcendentalist movement, when the philosophers of the Boston area were conducting experiments in new styles of life that broke with convention.

Walden Pond was not so wild; wilder places still exist near cities today. And the problems of the times were not much different than ours. The setting could be any time and any place and still make sense.

THEMES

1. ECONOMY

To Thoreau, the cost of something is not so much its actual cost in dollars and cents, but the amount of life that must be exchanged for it. A man is rich in proportion to the number of things he can let alone. Rather than accumulating things—possessions—Thoreau wanted the richness of time. His experiment in living at Walden Pond is an attempt to break away from the lives of desperation that he saw most people lead.

2. SLAVERY

Thoreau was an emphatic opponent of slavery. In fact, while living at Walden Pond he was arrested and jailed for failing to pay the $1 poll tax, a tax levied against anyone registered to vote. His refusal to pay was based on his refusal to support a government that tolerated—if not encouraged—slavery. (His aunt paid the tax and he was released from jail.) But even more prevalent at that time than the enslavement of blacks was everyone's enslavement to the material world—the world of *things*. At Walden Pond Thoreau found freedom.

3. TIME

Our lives are finite so we mustn't waste time on what is unnecessary, "As if you could kill time without injuring eternity," says Thoreau. At Walden Pond Thoreau lived according to what you might call "real time" or "natural time." His day was determined by the sun rising and setting, his years by the seasons.

He was not at the mercy of a structure imposed by the industrialized, so-called civilized world.

4. INDIVIDUALITY

Each man must search for his own path, and the search must take place within himself. "If a man does not keep pace with his companions, perhaps it is because he hears a different drummer. Let him step to the music which he hears, however measured or far away."

5. REBIRTH

The symbolism of rebirth is mirrored in the structure of the book, in which follows the changing seasons. Thoreau follows the process of decay and renewal as seen in the seasons and in the spiritual growth of a man.

6. COURAGE

Thoreau urges us to meet our lives, regardless of what they hold for us. Knowing is always better than not knowing. It is only through this courage that we may find our independent glory.

7. TRUTH

In his search for truth a man attains some measure of immortality that he can never achieve in any of his meaner pursuits. The wisdom of the ages is eternal life.

STYLE

The style of *Walden* owes a great deal to the way in which the material that makes up the book was first written. Thoreau kept a journal, not only while at Walden, but all his life. It was from the journal of his time at Walden Pond that he constructed the book. When keeping a journal, one tries to make an entry every day. This attempt to keep a daily account often results in brief jottings, and in changing quickly from one subject to another. This is evident when within a single chapter Thoreau switches from one topic to another.

Thoreau was concerned about his prose style. Listen to his description of ideal sentences: "Sentences which are expensive, towards which so many volumes, so much life, went; which lie like boulders on the page, up and down or across; which contain the seed of other sentences, not mere repetition, but creation; which a man might sell his grounds and castles to build." Thoreau's sentences were, indeed, expensive, distilled as they were from volume after volume of his journals. The fact that they are distilled, and that they were revised several times (there were at least six drafts of *Walden*) makes them seem concentrated, like nuggets. Thoreau tries to express universal truths, which often results in his sentences being like axioms, propositions accepted as self-evident truths, or being like epigrams. We have to read *Walden* only once to discover how many familiar quotations have been taken from its pages. It has been said that Thoreau was "a great craftsman whose trade was sentences."

POINT OF VIEW

There is never any question about whose point of view is being expressed in *Walden*. This is characteristic of literary compositions such as the essay, which usually deal with a subject from a personal point of view, and the journal or diary, which is a record of personal activities or feelings. You notice that the key word here is *personal*. In the second paragraph of *Walden* Thoreau says, "In most books, the *I*, or first per-

son, is omitted; in this it will be retained. . . . We
commonly do not remember that it is, after all, always
the first person that is speaking."

The voice you hear speaking in *Walden* is the voice
of a man who has lived an experiment. It is not the
voice of a "professor of philosophy," defined by Thoreau as one who merely "professes," but the voice of a
philosopher, a person who tries to solve some of the
problems of life "not only theoretically, but practi-
cally."

One function of Transcendentalism was the
attempt to influence society with the philosophies of
the movement. As a member of the movement Thoreau drew on his own experience to form conclusions
that apply to society as a whole. In many places in
Walden we find his worldview widening. From the
most distant horizon of his far shore to the village that
could be seen from the top of a nearby hill, his truths
could always be extended to society. You see his point
of view broaden from what he sees as his own sun,
moon, and stars, to what he sees as a sun that illuminates other worlds as well.

His ability to see and report on two levels lies in
what he describes as his "distance" or "doubleness."
In the chapter called "Solitude" he says, "I can stand
as remote from myself as from another. However
intense my experience, I am conscious of the presence
and criticism of a part of me, which, as it were, is not a
part of me, but spectator, sharing no experience, but
taking note of it." It is from this "doubleness" that he
derives his critical judgment. Remember that every
search, according to Thoreau, begins within the self.
Of this point of view he remarks, "I should not talk so
much about myself if there were any body else whom
I knew as well."

FORM AND STRUCTURE

Walden's form lies somewhere between the essay, a literary composition that considers its subject from a personal point of view, and the journal or diary, a daily account of personal activities and feelings. Its foundation is the journals Thoreau kept while at Walden, but he then elaborated on that material to set up larger arguments. Whereas Thoreau was actually at Walden Pond for a little over two years, the span of *Walden* is one year—from spring to spring. Hence it is more of an essay than a journal.

In its structure, *Walden* is organic. It follows the course of the natural year. Thoreau describes building his house in the spring, in the summer he moves to the pond, during the early fall he explores the surrounding area, in the winter he explores the area again. Finally we celebrate the return of spring, and the cycle is complete.

The Narrative

1. ECONOMY

The first chapter of *Walden* is the longest in the book. You will notice that every few pages there is extra space between two paragraphs. This is a signal that Thoreau is about to change the subject and begin a new section within the chapter. There are eleven such sections within this first chapter, "Economy." In the first section Thoreau introduces the book and begins his discussion of economy, or the management of one's expenses. He goes on in the second section to consider the necessities of life. In the third section he gives you a little background on himself and about how he came to live at Walden Pond. Clothing and shelter, respectively, are the subjects of the next two sections. In the sixth section Thoreau returns to a discussion of his beginnings at the pond and mentions the building of his cabin. This leads to a consideration of architecture in section seven. The cost of architectural improvements reminds Thoreau of a man's need to earn money, which is the subject of section eight. In section nine he describes the furnishings of his cabin. Section ten is a review of his experience in "maintaining" himself on earth. And in section eleven Thoreau gives his opinion of philanthropy, or humanitarianism—acts of good will toward one's fellow man.

Most of *Walden* was written between July 4, 1845 and September 6, 1847. Walden Pond is a mile from the nearest neighbor in the woods between Concord and Lincoln, near Boston, Massachusetts. Thoreau built his own house on the pond and earned his living there through manual labor.

Many people were curious about Thoreau's experiment in living, and asked him questions about everything from his diet to his fear of the woods. In part, *Walden* is an answer to those questions. It is written in the first person, and is the account of the person he knows best—himself.

Thoreau remarks, "I have travelled a good deal in Concord." This is one of his more famous—and humorous—lines, and he means by it that any exploration might best begin at home. What he has seen at home in Concord are his neighbors working, working so hard that they appear by their labor to be repenting for some terrible sin. The sight of them reminds Thoreau of Hindu peoples who subject themselves to torture, and of the labors of the mythological Hercules. The difference is that the people of Concord never seem to get anywhere for all their work. Thoreau pities young people who have inherited property and possessions, saying that these things are harder to get rid of than they are to acquire. These people do little more than dig their own graves during their lifetimes. Thoreau describes them in pathetic images, first as burdened by the belongings that they must push ahead of themselves on the road of life, then as having hands that have grown too clumsy and rough from work to pick the fruits of life that require the most delicate handling. He sees people as being on a treadmill, leading what he calls "lives of quiet desperation." People seem resigned to their fate when, in fact, it is what a man thinks of *himself* that largely determines the course of his life. That is, man can determine his fate rather than be a victim of it. Thoreau warns us against taking anyone else's word for what we should do or even can do. The old, he says, speak from experience, but their experience is often one of failure. It is never too late to change.

As an example of the kind of advice that is the result of faulty reasoning and is worthless to us, Thoreau tells a story. A farmer told him that a vegetarian diet is unsound because it supplies nothing that the body can use in making bones. Thoreau adds that the farmer is saying this as he walks behind a plow drawn by his oxen whose enormously strong bones and muscles pull it through the rough ground. The oxen eat only vegetable material—so much for the farmer's reasoning! This first section ends with Thoreau quoting the Chinese philosopher Confucius, who says that true knowledge is knowing what we do and do not know.

In the second section Thoreau questions the necessities of life. By going back in time (either in practical terms by leading a more primitive life-style or in historical terms to the records left by traders and merchants) we get a sense of what is truly necessary. To some creatures it is only food; to others it is food and shelter. For man in this climate it is food, shelter, clothing, and fuel; it is not until a man has the things that he needs that he feels the freedom to consider other problems of life. Since we have outgrown the savage state we have lost our ability to live as savages, to be warm while naked. "Heat is life," says Thoreau. Our food is actually just fuel to heat our bodies; our clothing and shelter help us to retain the body heat.

Thoreau itemizes his other necessities: a knife, an axe, a spade, a wheelbarrow, lamplight, stationery, and access to a few books. Many of our comforts are like ballast weighing us down when we try to "elevate" ourselves or achieve a higher state. In many and varied cultures we find examples of philosophers who were, by our standards, very poor. But it was always by choice; they chose to do without and to lead simple lives so that nothing would distract them from their thoughts. Thoreau suggests that only from such a position of "voluntary poverty" can a person observe life fairly and with an uncluttered, unobstructed view.

In an extended metaphor for a man as a plant, Thoreau asks why would we put down roots into the earth if we were not planning to grow as far in the direction of heaven as we grow into the earth. After all, he figures, plants are valued for the fruit they produce above ground. Thoreau closes this section saying that he is speaking not to those who mind their business and take care of themselves, but to those who are discontented with their lives, especially those who are considered "wealthy" but who are imprisoned by their chains of silver and gold.

The third section is a brief account of Thoreau's life before Walden, not of specific events, but of aspects of his character and personality that made him a likely candidate for the experiment. He speaks of himself here as if he were describing a character from a fable. You understand that he has concentrated all his attention on Nature, as when he says that he tried to hear what was in the wind, or that he waited at evening for the sky to fall so that he might catch a piece of it. He claims that his position was that of "self-appointed inspector of snow-storms and rain-storms," and surveyor of ravines and forest paths. He also says that he helped the sun in rising by being there when it did. You understand how he sees himself in the grand scheme of things when he says that he is "anxious to stand at the meeting of two eternities, past and future, which is precisely the present moment."

In this almost cosmic language Thoreau raises his own life to the level of myth in an obscure but often quoted paragraph:

I long ago lost a hound, a bay horse, and a turtle dove, and am still on their trail. Many are the travellers I have spoken concerning them, describing their tracks and what calls they answered to. I have met one or two who had heard the hound, and the tramp of the horse, and even seen the dove disappear behind a cloud, and they seemed as anxious to recover them as if they had lost them themselves.

The lost creatures here are symbols of those things in life which we can never capture but are always searching for.

Section four is Thoreau's discourse on clothing. In his mind clothing serves no purpose other than retaining heat and covering nakedness. He dismisses novelty and fashion and criticizes those who care more about their clothes than about the person inside them. He warns us against new activity that requires new clothes—rather than a new "wearer of clothes." He then compares us with animals who molt. We should change our clothes at a turning point in our lives so that we will not be like new wine in old bottles. But of course simply changing our clothes will not change us.

In the fifth section Thoreau goes on to discuss his philosophy of another necessity, shelter. We should try to get by with as little shelter as possible; after all, birds do not sing in caves. It is in this section that we hear one of the basic principles of Thoreau's economy: "The cost of something is the amount of life which is required to be exchanged for it, immediately or in the long run," and Thoreau is sickened by the amount of life exchanged for the rental of a house or the mortgage on a farm. The solution to an economic problem is often more complex than the problem itself, as when a farmer deals in herds of cattle in order to have enough money to buy shoelaces. Housing is like clothing—*it* improves, but not those who are inside. Thoreau describes what we now call "keeping up with the Joneses," and complains about how possessions complicate life. He himself kept three pieces of limestone on his desk until he realized that they needed to be dusted every day, at which point he threw them away in disgust. Even on the railroad, money is spent on the wrong things—more on luxury than on safety. In a famous line Thoreau remarks that he would rather sit on a pumpkin and have it all to himself than be crowded on a velvet cushion.

NOTE: In this section you will notice a reference to someone named "Jonathan." In the mid 1800s this was a name used to refer to any American, and the name "John" was used to refer to any Englishman. It is similar to referring to an average person today as "John Doe." Keep this in mind, because Thoreau will make use of these names later in the book.

Halfway through the first chapter section six begins. Thoreau explains that in March of 1845 he borrowed an axe and went down to the site of his house and began to cut down timber. It is important to note that the cycle at Walden Pond begins here, in the spring. Thoreau recalls seeing a snake slip out of the leaves and into some icy water and stay there, paralyzed. He compares the snake to men who live in a spiritual winter and do not feel the effects of spring in their souls.

NOTE: The song that he sings to himself here, like all the poems that appear in the text without quotation marks, was written by Thoreau.

As they were needed, Thoreau borrowed more tools. He worked all spring on his house, framing it with boards bought and taken from the shack of one James Collins, an Irish railroad worker. The house was raised in May with help from neighbors. Thoreau moved in on the fourth of July.

Section seven alternates between Thoreau's thoughts on architecture in general and reports on his own cabin in particular. He goes back to the subject of ornaments; beauty in architecture, he says, is a function of purpose and usefulness and not appearance or ornament.

Before winter set in he was able to build his chimney, to shingle, and to plaster. The house was 10 feet wide by 15 feet long, had a garret (an attic), a closet, a large window on either side, the door at one end and the fireplace at the other. With leftover materials, he built a small woodshed out back.

For the amount a man spends on rent in one year, he could own his own shelter, says Thoreau. He discusses the high cost of room, board, and tuition at colleges, and says we learn more by doing than by studying, experience alone makes for productive time. The tragedy of our lives is that we spend our best years earning money so that we can have free time when we are old, when the time is of little value to us.

While working on his house Thoreau found himself in need of around $10 to meet expenses. To generate income, he planted beans, potatoes, corn, peas, and

turnips. Not only was it cheaper to use a spade to turn
the ground than to hire a team of oxen to plow, this
also kept him independent. We think of men as the
keeper of herds, but herds can also be keepers of men
and are, in a way, much freer.

By farming ($23.44) and by doing a little carpentry
and surveying ($13.34), Thoreau earned $36.78 in a
year. His expenses were $61.99 and ¾ of a cent. He
made up the difference with money he already had
when he started.

He admits that he is thinking more of economy
than of diet when he suggests that men should eat as
simply as the animals and not trouble themselves so
much in getting food. If each of us could raise his own
food and build his own shelter, all trade in these two
necessities of life could be eliminated.

In the ninth section Thoreau itemizes the furnishings of his house, some of which he made himself: a
bed, a table, a desk, three chairs, a looking glass (3" in
diameter), a pair of tongs and andirons for the fire, a
kettle, a skillet, a frying pan, a ladle, a washbowl, two
knives, and two forks, three plates, one cup, one
spoon, a jug for oil, a jug for molasses, and a lamp.
Curtains were unnecessary since only the sun and
moon looked in. Thoreau says in this section that if
you have to drag your trap, it had better be a light
one.

In section ten Thoreau speaks from his own experience in earning his living. He claims that he was able
to support himself for five years by doing manual
labor only six weeks a year. This left all of the winter
and most of the summer free for study and reading.
He lists as his greatest skill the fact that he wanted
little and that he valued his freedom more than fine
furniture, carpets, delicate food, or a fancy house. He
has nothing to say to people who work for the sake of

working. They are so enslaved that they wouldn't know what to do with more free time. Supporting ourselves should be a pastime rather than a hardship. We should live wisely and simply and in as many different ways as there are people.

The tone of the chapter's final section is sometimes puzzling and difficult to understand. You have been listening to a man tell you how to improve your life. And yet here he criticizes those who try to improve the lives of others, saying that charity is an overrated virtue. Thoreau is reacting here to a sad fact of philanthropy (good will to others) that continues today. Much "goodness" is motivated by guilt or fear and, as such, is "tainted." Thoreau says that if you want to "restore mankind by . . . natural means" you should be "as simple and well as Nature" herself. It is a theme you will hear again and again in the book.

2. WHERE I LIVED, AND WHAT I LIVED FOR

Chapter 2 is as straightforward as its title sounds. It first gives a description of the site of Thoreau's cabin, and then the reasons why he lived as he did. In many ways it is a shorter and more moving version of his first chapter on "Economy."

Before showing you the very spot where he built his house, Thoreau gives you a little background on his experiences in the local real estate market. He knows the countryside well. In his mind, he's bought every farm within a radius of twelve miles, and has discovered many homesites in the undeveloped landscape as well. He says, "At a certain season of our life we are accustomed to consider every spot as the possible site of a house." He's telling you now of his experiences in that period of his own life.

It may surprise you to learn how close Thoreau came to buying a farm in Concord known as the Hollowell place. He remembered the farm from his first trips up the Sudbury River. He liked it for its hollow apple trees, its dilapidated fences, its run-down gray house, and its location two miles from the village and a half mile from any neighbor. The farmer's wife changed her mind about selling at the last minute, just before Thoreau had been given a deed to the property. All this happened before Thoreau decided to go to Walden Pond. If the deal had not fallen through, the commitment of owning and operating a big farm might have kept Thoreau from his experiment in essential living. Both his name and the name of Walden Pond might be unknown to us today. In thinking back on how close he'd come to owning a farm of his own, Thoreau offers a bit of wisdom: you live free and uncommitted as long as possible, because in the long run it doesn't matter if you are trapped by your responsibilities or by the county jail. And in any event, it isn't actually necessary to own a piece of land in order to gain the spiritual joys it has to offer.

Thoreau claims it was quite by accident that he began his life in the woods on Independence Day. When he began spending his nights there, the house was not yet finished. It was little more than a shelter from the rain. The walls were not plastered, but were rough boards with wide spaces in between through which air passed, keeping the cabin cool in the summer evenings. The hewn wood of the studs and the planed door and window casings gave the place a clean look, and the unfinished nature of the inside gave the cabin a sketchy quality. There was no need for Thoreau to go outside to get air because the atmosphere inside was still so fresh. (You will see him make the place fit for the winter in the chapter called

"House-Warming.") He felt that he had caged himself nearer the birds whose songs were familiar to him, and to those that were never heard in the village.

Thoreau describes the setting of his cabin in the woods. The cabin was by the shore of Walden, a small pond. It was situated at such a low point that the opposite shore of Walden Pond was the most distant horizon—Thoreau could see nothing past that. He describes the water in the pond during a break in a rainstorm in August, when the surface is smooth and full of light and reflection. It seems suspended like a heaven hanging lower than the sky. Although from a certain nearby hilltop Thoreau could see distant peaks ranging from a near green to a distant blue, and some portion of the village, in other directions he could not see over or beyond the woods.

You might feel crowded or confined by the restricted view. But for Thoreau it was as if he had entered a warp in time and space. He felt as far away from the life he'd left behind as if he were in a constellation in the night sky seen only by astronomers—a new and untouched place in the universe. He seemed closer to times past, times in history that had always appealed to him. The heroic ages seemed revived even in his daily practice of awakening early and bathing in the pond—a ritual of renewal recommended since the time of Confucius.

Many writers have praised morning; Thoreau joins them, calling it "the most memorable season of the day." For him it is a magical time, a time when you have an intelligence or consciousness that you have at no other time of the day. For him the words *awake* and *alive* have the same meaning. The atmosphere of morning, the atmosphere of hope and infinite expectation, is one you should try to carry with you, making the rest of your life worthy of these best hours.

It was just this sort of striving—a striving to improve his life by living as simply as possible—that led Thoreau to the woods. He hoped to learn from that simplicity what is essential in life, and to experience it. You know what Thoreau means when he says "life is frittered away by detail." Life, in his view, has become like a country growing up without a plan into a cluttered and unwieldy mess. People are in too much of a hurry, and are always wasting time. They're concerned with news that is little more than gossip, instead of trying to learn more about more abiding truths. In our more unhurried moments we have a better perspective from which to evaluate what is important and what is petty in life. Thoreau urges you to spend one day as deliberately as Nature, and not be distracted from that task by anything but reality. Back to basics.

The chapter ends with one of the book's better-known and often-quoted passages:

> Time is but the stream I go a-fishing in. I drink at it; but while I drink I see the sandy bottom and detect how shallow it is. Its thin current slides away, but eternity remains. I would drink deeper; fish in the sky, whose bottom is pebbly with stars.

NOTE: This is a good example of the more difficult but exciting passages in *Walden*. It uses metaphor to push a thought as far as it can be imagined. It is a passage that *must* and *can* be read again and again, and even once you understand it, you would have a hard time explaining it exactly to someone else. This is why it is exciting—because it remains mysterious.

---

3. READING

In this chapter you learn Thoreau's thoughts about reading. It is a short chapter, and all of a piece. No sights or sounds filter in from the outdoors to distract Thoreau from the theme at hand.

We learn right away, in the first paragraph, that when Thoreau says "reading" he means the serious reading of serious books. It occurs to him that all people would probably become students if they thought about it long enough, because one thing that all people share is a desire to learn the truth. In trying to satisfy this desire (through reading) we achieve a kind of immortality that we cannot achieve by acquiring property or by starting a family or, even, by building a reputation. This desire for truth, as he describes it, acts almost as an independent force, and connects all people. He makes it sound like a single thread running through everyone. In a haunting and exotic metaphor for writing and reading, Thoreau describes an ancient philosopher "raising a corner of the veil from the statue of divinity." The veil remains raised so Thoreau can see the statue in the way the philosopher did. The desire for truth is the same in both of these men, and it is what makes them do what they do: it makes the philosopher think and write about wisdom and knowledge, and it makes the student read the philosopher's writings.

Completing his house, and having to hoe his fields all the time, kept Thoreau from doing any serious reading during his first summer at Walden Pond. But the spot was a good one for reading and thinking, and Thoreau kept a copy of Homer's *Iliad* on the table all the while. It served as a reminder of what he had to look forward to when the greater part of his manual labor was done.

But you must not misunderstand him here, he does not think of reading as an easy activity that entertains you after you have spent the better part of your energy and attention on something else. Thoreau considers reading one of the most demanding endeavors a person can undertake. He says that "to read well, that is, to read true books in a true spirit, is a noble exercise." He compares the training it requires to the training that athletes undergo. And he recommends that books be read as carefully as they were written.

NOTE: One of the biggest problems we have in understanding the classics comes from having to read them in English translation. Thoreau suggests that every student learn even a few words of an ancient language, if only to get a taste of its special flavor. When we read books that have been translated from another language, we should keep that fact in mind and try to imagine what larger meaning the words might have had in other times and in other places. It is not enough to be able to *speak* in the original language, for there is a world of difference between a language as it is spoken and that same language as it is written.

Thoreau's opinion of this difference between the spoken and the written word is summed up in two similes, or comparisons. Words that are spoken are like clouds. They are fleeting; they don't last. Written words, on the other hand, are like the stars—fixtures in the heavens. They can be studied and commented on forever by anyone who can understand them.

The written word is the work of art that's closest to life itself. It doesn't need marble or canvas in order to exist. It can even escape the confines of paper, and exist in human breath itself (that is, we can read it and repeat it aloud), and in every language. Writers become influential in all societies. For evidence that intellectual culture is desirable, you have only to look at your own society. Uneducated people who make a great deal of money in business are not satisfied to be admitted to wealthy and fashionable circles. They want still more. They want their children to attend the very best schools so that *they* may someday be admitted to the still higher circles of intellectual culture. Thoreau emphasizes this idea of *ascending* when he claims that the classics and scriptures of the many nations of the earth are the prizes and trophies of the centuries. He imagines these volumes stacked up like a flight of stairs that may lead us to heaven, at last.

He returns to his image of written words as stars in the heavens when he talks about the works of the great poets. Reading them is more like astrology, the occult study of the influence the stars might have on our horoscopes, than like astronomy, which is a serious science of the heavenly bodies. We read, he says, for the sake of convenience. We do this in the same way that we learn and remember just enough math so that we won't be cheated when we buy things. We seem satisfied to read books that don't require much thought, or to read condensed versions of stories or romances about characters with such unlikely names as Zebulon and Sophronia. He gets quite carried away mimicking the ridiculous story line that such romances follow.

Even good readers, Thoreau complains, don't read the best books. The person who has just finished reading an English classic can't find anyone to talk to about it. These classics are golden words and no one goes near them. But every one of you would go out of your way to pick up a silver dollar.

Living with great books and not reading them isn't much different from living next door to someone and never meeting that person. And if those of you who *can* read *don't* read, then you are no different from those who can't read at all. You probably "soar but little higher in [your] intellectual flights than the columns of the daily paper."

"Not all books are as dull as their readers," he continues. If you could understand them, there are some books that address your condition exactly and may at times mean more to you than morning or spring itself. How often have you begun an explanation with the words, "I don't know how to say this. . . "? Chances are there is a book somewhere that says it for you. Because the same questions come up again and again, in each age different authors offer answers in their own words.

The problem of being undereducated and illiterate is not one that Thoreau sees as beginning and ending with the individual. The village of Concord does as little for its culture as any one man does for his own intellectual growth. If progress were measured by amounts of money spent on school systems, then there would be little sign of progress in the nineteenth century. People stop their formal education as soon as they stop being children. Villages should be like universities, or take the place of the noblemen of Europe as patrons of the arts. This is a familiar complaint in our age. "This town has spent seventeen thousand dollars on a town-house, thank fortune or politics, but probably it will not spend so much on living wit . . . in a hundred years."

In closing Thoreau suggests some town planning that would make the changes possible: "If it is necessary, omit one bridge over the river, go round a little there, and throw one arch at least over the darker gulf of ignorance which surrounds us."

4. SOUNDS

This chapter has three distinct sections. In the first Thoreau, being a true Transcendentalist, urges you to experience life directly, through nature, rather than chiefly through books. In the second you find him interrupted by the sound of the railroad, trying to integrate that unnatural sound with his natural world. In the third the sound of the railroad dies away and Thoreau is left, very much alone, with the sounds and the language of nature.

If you wanted to know if a person could understand the Spanish language, you would probably ask, " Do you speak Spanish?" All over the world the term *to speak* a language is used to mean *to understand*. But in order to understand a language we must also be able to listen.

What worries Thoreau is that people are forgetting the language of Nature. After all he has just said about the importance of reading books, it's as if he now wants to add, "But don't get me wrong, books are not the best source of knowledge." More important than any course in history or poetry is the ability to see what is to be seen, simply to be aware of the world around you. This, too, requires study.

His own method of study was simple: he sat in his doorway and listened, unaware of the passing of time. This was his work. The townspeople thought he was lazy, but Thoreau preferred to be judged not by the standards of other men, but by the standards of birds and flowers. He says, "The natural day is very calm, and will hardly reprove his indolence."

Unlike most people, Thoreau didn't feel as if he had to go to the theater, for instance, and to be around other people in order to have a good time. He seemed to have a good time no matter what he was doing; most people would call it looking on the bright side of things. But Thoreau even enjoyed cleaning out his little cabin. He enjoyed seeing his table and chairs out on the grass amid the trees. He thought they seemed glad to get outside. It seemed right to have the natural forms returned to the natural surroundings that inspired them.

While Thoreau is sitting at his window he hears the rattle of railroad cars, the sound coming and going in the air like the sound of a wingbeat. It is the Fitchburg Railroad, which runs about a hundred yards from his cabin. Its tracks are the path that he follows into town.

NOTE: When you read his descriptions of the railroad, note his vision, his way of looking at the world. Everything he looks at he sees in terms of natural imagery. When he describes the train it appears first as a comet visiting our solar system. Then it is a magnificent iron horse, snorting thunder and breathing fire and smoke. For him the railroad is like the sun; it is as regular in its motions. Farmers set their clocks by the sound of its whistle. Men are more punctual because of it. Life is faster because of it. This single industry influences the whole country, but interferes with the life of no one. It is like a powerful creature with a mind of its own.

The coming of the railroad is the coming of a commerce that braves the gravest weather in its exchange of exotic palm leaf, hemp, and coconut husks from foreign land for lumber, rags, and fish from New England. And when the cattle train passes, it sounds like a whole valley going by.

But all the natural images in the world cannot conceal Thoreau's true feelings about the railroad. In any disguise it is still a symbol of the commerce and industry that signals the end of an agricultural society. It signifies the end of a harmony between man and the natural world. It is still a symbol of the Industrial Revolution, of factory work and low wages for some and a new breed of materialism for others. The sense we have after reading this passage is one of sadness, for the cattle herders who are left without a job. We also mourn our own "pastoral life whirled past and away."

You have probably noticed how quiet it seems when a very loud noise suddenly stops. In that hush, when Thoreau can no longer hear the railroad cars and feel their rumbling, he feels more alone than ever. He hears only the faint rattle of a far-off carriage or team of horses, or on Sundays the churchbells from neighboring towns. But note the quality of that sound coming from such a great distance: it speaks of each leaf and pine needle it passes on its way to you. As it travels it becomes the voice of the woods.

The lowing of a cow, the evening prayer of the whip-poor-wills, the wail of the screech owl (*Oh-o-o-o-o that I never had been bor-r-r-n!"*), and the changing howls of the hooting owls give a voice to the dismal twilight woods. The evening has another voice: the rumble of distant wagons over bridges, the baying of dogs, and the trumpeting questions of bullfrogs ("*tr-r-r-oonk, tr-r-r-oonk, tr-r-r-oonk!*") and their answer ("*troonk*").

What he doesn't remember hearing is the sound of a cock, whose note is the most remarkable of any bird. It is his fantasy that this once wild bird might live as a native in these woods, filling the air with his song. But like so many other domestic sounds—the sounds of dogs, cats, hens, pigs, even tea kettles—the note of the cock is missing from Thoreau's yard. In fact, he has no yard. There is only the wilderness growing up around him.

NOTE: When reading about the absence of the cock or chanticleer, you might want to think back to the epigraph of the book in which Thoreau says, "I do not propose to write an ode to dejection, but to brag as lustily as chanticleer in the morning, standing on his roost, if only to wake my neighbors up."

---

5. SOLITUDE

It is still evening when this next chapter begins, and you can still hear the bullfrogs and the whip-poor-wills. Thoreau describes a freedom that he feels in Nature, which gives him the sense of being a part of Nature herself.

Returning to his cabin after a walk, Thoreau can always tell when someone has stopped by in his absence. If not from a calling card, a note, or a bunch of flowers, he can tell by the bended twigs or grass, by a footprint, or by the lingering odor of cigar or pipe smoke.

His nearest neighbor is only a mile away; the railroad passes on one side of Walden Pond, and the woodland road between Concord and Lincoln on the other. Yet he feels as solitary there as if he were on the prairies. He may as well be in Africa or Asia; he has the sun, moon, and stars all to himself. At night he gets no more traffic past his house than if he were the first or last man on earth.

He admits that there was one time, just a few weeks after arriving at Walden, when he felt lonely. He says he wondered then if close neighbors were a requirement for a healthy and serene life. The feeling lasted about an hour. Then, suddenly, in everything he could see and hear, even in the drops of rain, he sensed what he calls an "unaccountable friendliness." He felt befriended even by the little pine needles of the woods. At that moment his feeling of loneliness vanished. Human neighbors no longer mattered, and they haven't mattered since.

If you had met Thoreau while he was living at Walden Pond you might have been one of the many people who asked if he felt lonely, especially when it rained or snowed. Thoreau answers this question with another question. What sort of space is it that separates one person from another? Is it physical space? There is no physical movement that can bring together two minds that have a difference of opinion. We are often more lonely among others than we are when we stay alone in our rooms. "Society is commonly too cheap. We meet at very short intervals, not having had time to acquire any new value for each other. We meet at meals three times a day, and give each other a new taste of that old musty cheese that we are." This closeness, this frequency, Thoreau says, makes us lose respect for each other.

No matter where he is, a person who's working or thinking is always alone. Thinking, in fact, creates distance in two ways—distance from others and distance from ourselves. You have no doubt worked in a crowded and busy library or study hall. You have probably noticed that no matter how many other people surrounded you, in your thoughts you are essentially alone. In thinking you also achieve a distance from yourself. You can consciously stand apart from your actions and their consequences. There is a part of you, no matter how intense the experience, that is always the spectator. That part of you does not share in, but merely notes the experience.

As a part of nature Thoreau felt great harmony with his surroundings. And as a part of nature he was no more lonely than a loon in a pond is lonely. He was no more lonely than a dandelion, a horsefly, the North Star, the South wind, an April shower, or Walden Pond itself.

6. VISITORS

You have already noticed how Thoreau uses one chapter to balance another. This chapter on "Visitors" acts to balance the chapter on "Solitude." It does so in the same way that the chapter on "Sounds" acted to balance the chapter on "Reading."

Thoreau claims to love society as much as the next person. He says that he is not a hermit by nature. In the chapter entitled "Economy" he told us that he had three chairs in his cabin. Here he tells us what each of the three chairs symbolizes in his life: "one for solitude, two for friendship, three for society." When he was visited in greater numbers (sometimes by twenty-five or thirty people at once) everyone stood. On the subject of being part of a large group, he has a thought that is probably familiar to you. He says that after being together, "we often parted without being aware that we had come very near to one another." You hear repeated a theme from "Solitude"—that we are often most alone when among others.

In a small space you complain of feeling "on top of one another." Thoreau describes this feeling he has when he is confined with other people. But his reasons for this feeling are probably different from yours. For him a conversation is the unfolding of thoughts. In his mind these thoughts need room to travel and come to rest before being appreciated by others. It is as if he imagines thoughts as things that can be visualized, like paintings. You know how hard it is to see a large painting if you are standing up close to it. He describes two people speaking thoughtfully in a small space as two stones thrown into a pool of still water, thrown so close together that they interfere with each other's radiating waves.

NOTE: In the mid-1800s every house had a drawing room—a room that we might now call a living room—where guests were entertained. Thoreau, on the other hand, had what he called his "withdrawing room." It was the pine wood behind the cabin, and it was always ready for guests, its floor swept and furniture dusted by the wind.

More people came to visit Thoreau while he was at Walden Pond than at any other time in his life. Many were simply curious, although the numbers were kept down by his distance from the village.

One of the people he encountered often was a Canadian woodchopper and post maker, a man who fascinated Thoreau. He was so humble that humility did not seem a distinct quality in him. He was not at all sophisticated. Thoreau says that he would no more think of introducing this man to his neighbor than he would think of introducing a woodchuck to his neighbor—he had to be found out. In his quiet, solitary, and humble life, this man was happy. Thoreau says

that a "more natural man would be hard to find."
And yet, it seems, his natural man had a flaw. Thoreau defines it by saying that "the intellectual and
spiritual man in him were slumbering, like an infant."
He remained no more than a highly developed animal—although close to nature, still no ideal man.

Thoreau briefly mentions other visitors: the poor,
children, the mentally disturbed, a runaway slave,
ministers, doctors, lawyers, and reformers, "the
greatest bores of all." Thoreau welcomes them all, but
nowhere do we find the same enthusiasm he
expressed in his own company. Perhaps we must
think again of his claim that he is no hermit, after all.

7. THE BEAN-FIELD

In the second paragraph in this chapter Thoreau
recalls the day he first saw Walden Pond. It was when
he was four years old. His family was living in Boston
at the time, and returned to Concord, the town of
Henry's birth, for a visit. They passed through the
very woods where he would later live, and went to
the pond. The sight of it is a scene he remembers well;
it is one of the oldest stamped on his memory. In this
chapter he reviews that scene, the same pines, almost
the same johnswort. What's changed is that he can
now see his influence, the result of his presence on
the landscape, and this is the bean-field.

His is the only cultivated field for quite a stretch in
every direction. It is the subject of comments from
passersby on the woodland road. It is two and a half
acres in size. The rows of beans, measured end-to-end
and added together, are seven miles long. His helpers
are the fertility of the soil and the rain and dew that
water the soil. He uses no manure. His only tool is a
hoe. His enemies are woodchucks, worms, and cold

days. Using primitive methods he's slower than most
farmers, but closer to the earth. Husbandry—that is,
planting, hoeing, harvesting, threshing, picking over,
and selling the beans—was his "curious labor all summer." He harvested twelve bushels and made a profit
of $8.71½. And he was wildly happy doing so.

NOTE: Working the bean-field made Thoreau
not unlike Antaeus, the mythological figure who
derived his strength from touching the earth, and
who was killed when Hercules held him off the
ground. As he hoes, Thoreau overturns arrowheads
and bits of pottery, the remains of other, earlier farmers and hunters. Ancient poetry tells us that husbandry was once a sacred art. Now the farmer has the
meanest of lives.

The bean-field at Walden Pond is a "connecting link
between wild and cultivated fields." Thoreau's labor
affords him a long acquaintanceship with the land,
and his kinship with nature is accompanied by the
music of his hoe tinkling against the stones, the song
of the brown thrasher, and the sound of the heavens
rent by a swooping hawk.

In many ways the bean-field is a symbol for Thoreau himself. He embodies and enjoys the wildness of
nature and the discipline and cultivation of civilization. He lives in a state that we might call "human
nature," if that term hadn't come to mean something
else entirely.

8. THE VILLAGE

We find Thoreau bathing again, this time after a
morning spent hoeing or reading and writing. It was
part of his routine to go into the village of Concord

every day or two to listen to the gossip, which he found—in very small doses—to be "as refreshing in its way as the rustle of leaves and the peeping of frogs." The villagers are a curiosity to him, yet another subject for study. The woods offer him a setting in which he can see squirrels and birds. The village offers him a setting in which he can see men and boys.

By comparison, the village emerges as a much more threatening environment than the woods. Thoreau describes a walk down a residential street lined with houses as "running the gauntlet," which means passing between two rows of men armed with sticks while they try to strike you. Even the shopkeepers' signs are a dangerous lure, appealing as they do to a man's appetite or fancy. Thoreau manages to escape the dangers either by walking boldly past them or by fixing his mind on other and higher matters. He compares himself to Orpheus, the figure in Greek mythology whose singing drowns out the sound of the sirens who were trying to lure him into dangerous waters.

His escape from the village is, not surprisingly, to the woods. He describes some of his absentminded trips through that darkness, feeling with his feet a path that his eyes cannot see. To be lost in the woods, he says, is a surprising, memorable, and valuable experience. It isn't until he's completely lost that he can appreciate how vast and strange nature is.

Discussion of the village gives Thoreau an occasion to mention his most famous visit to Concord. On that day he was arrested and jailed for refusing to pay the $1 poll tax. He says he would not "recognize the authority of the State which buys and sells men, women, and children, like cattle." In other words, he would not support a government that allowed slavery.

NOTE: It was this incident that led to the other work for which Thoreau is well known, his essay, "On the Duty of Civil Disobedience."

In all his time at Walden Pond, Thoreau isn't bothered by anyone except those representing the government. Although he is away from his cabin much of the time, he has no need to lock his door. Except for one book by Homer, nothing is ever stolen from him. It is his belief that "robbery and thieving" would disappear altogether if everyone lived as simply as he.

The subject of crime leads to the subject of punishment. The chapter ends with a quote from Confucius, addressing those who work for the government.

> You who govern public affairs, what need have you to employ punishments? Love virtue, and the people will be virtuous. The virtues of a superior man are like the wind; the virtues of a common man are like the grass; the grass, when the wind passes over it, bends.

It is a plea to the state to govern by example. It is a very idealistic philosophy, which echoes the motto with which Thoreau opens his essay on civil disobedience—"That government is best which governs least."

NOTE: Notice how in some ways this chapter is like the chapter entitled "Visitors." In both chapters Thoreau assumes a positive stance. He claims a high regard for his subject, which in both cases is other people. Then as the chapter progresses you hear little but criticism of that subject. "Visitors" exposes the limitations of the individual, and "The Village" shows the limitations of a group of individuals or a society.

9. THE PONDS

In the short section that introduces this chapter Thoreau tells us some of the activities he enjoyed when he'd had enough of people and gossip. Picking huckleberries and blueberries in the hills to the west was a favorite. The picker, and no one else, knows the flavor of these fruits, for it is lost in their trip to market. Fishing, too, is a pleasant pastime. On occasion he joins others who are fishing at Walden. At other times he fishes alone in the moonlight. Like the bean-field, the fishing line is seen as a link, another connection between spiritual and natural worlds.

> It was very queer, especially in dark nights, when your thoughts had wandered to vast and cosmog-onal themes [theories regarding the origin of the universe] in other spheres, to feel this faint jerk, which came to interrupt your dreams and link you to Nature again. It seemed as if I might next cast my line upward into the air, as well as downward into this element, which was scarcely more dense. Thus I caught two fishes as it were with one hook.

NOTE: This will remind you of the paragraph that ends Chapter 2, which begins, "Time is but the stream I go a-fishing in."

The next section comprises about three-quarters of the chapter. It is a detailed description of the most important feature in Thoreau's landscape: a description of Walden Pond and its physical setting. Walden is a half-mile long and a mile and three-quarters around, containing an area of sixty-one-and-a-half acres. The woodland hills that surround it rise up to a height of forty to eighty feet.

The color of the pond is the subject of much discussion. In some cases the color seems to depend on the light, and reflect the sky. In others it seems to repeat the colors found on land. Thoreau's description of this phenomenon suggests again that Walden is a place between worlds, one natural and one devine: "Lying between the earth and the heavens, it partakes of the color of both." In quality, the water is pure and clear and transparent even at a depth of thirty feet. Thoreau recalls a time when he dropped his axe through a hole in the ice at Walden, and was able to find it and fish it off the bottom of the pond, the water was so clear.

Except for one or two little sandy beaches, a belt of smooth and rounded white stones make up the shore. Thoreau mentions a few of the theories of how such regular paving came about. The shore is cleanest when the water is lowest, but it is the high water that keeps it clean as if the lake were licking its lips from time to time. This rising and falling of the water level is a fluctuation that takes place over the course of years.

NOTE: In light of the metaphor of the pond for a man's spirit, you should take note of this rising and falling of the water level. It will be mentioned again in the concluding chapter of the book.

Perch, pouts, shiners, chivins, breams, eels, and three kinds of pickerel are among the fish that have been caught at Walden. While the pond is "not very fertile in fish," the fish that swim here are "cleaner, handsomer, and firmer-fleshed than those in the river and most other ponds." Its animal population includes frogs, tortoises, muskrats, minks, mud turtles, ducks, geese, white-bellied swallows, kingfishers, peetweets, fish hawks, and a single loon.

In the second half of this section Thoreau discusses the relation a body of water has to the rest of the landscape of nature. He uses the words *pond* and *lake* interchangeably to refer to Walden. As Walden is often viewed as a symbol of Thoreau's spirit in this book, you should take note of these descriptions that offer great clues to Thoreau's ideas and ideals.

In a carefully drawn image Thoreau describes the lake as the most beautiful and expressive feature of a landscape. "It is the earth's eye; looking into which the beholder measures the depth of his own nature. The fluviatile trees next the shore are the slender eyelashes which fringe it, and the wooded hills and cliffs around are its overhanging brows." The image of the lake as an instrument for spiritual *vision* continues after a paragraph about its grassy surface, when he says:

> Walden is a perfect forest mirror. . . . Sky water
> . . . . It is a mirror which no stone can crack, whose quicksilver will never wear off, whose gilding Nature continually repairs; no storms, no dust, can dim its surface ever fresh;—a mirror in which all impurity presented to it sinks, . . . which retains no breath that is breathed on it, but sends its own to float as clouds high above its surface, and be reflected in its bosom still.

Again, he draws the link,

> A Field of water betrays the spirit that is in the air
> . . . . It is intermediate in its nature between land and sky.

The wooded hills surrounding Walden have been cleared in places by woodchoppers. Instead of going to Walden to drink or to bathe, the villagers are now thinking of piping its water into Concord. Thoreau imagines them washing their dishes with it. The railroad—represented again as an Iron Horse, a terrible beast—has muddied a nearby bubbling spring, and here a track for it has been cleared through the woods on one shore. And yet Walden survives and is essentially unchanged: "Of all the characters I have known . . . Walden wears best." It is always young. What changes is Thoreau.

In the last lines of this section on Walden Thoreau reminds you that the pond had no visible inlet or outlet. He acknowledges that it must be related to Flint's Pond nearby, but despairs at the thought of the two ponds ever being reconnected. In these lines he gives us another indication that Walden is a symbol for his own spirit, when he describes it in words that you might use to describe him: "living thus reserved and austere, like a hermit in the woods, so long, it has acquired such wonderful purity."

In the last quarter of the chapter Thoreau mentions four other ponds nearby: Flint's, or Sandy Pond, in Lincoln a mile east of Walden; Goose Pond, between Concord and Lincoln; Fair-Haven, an expansion of the Concord River, one mile southeast; and White Pond, a mile and a half beyond that.

Most of what Thoreau has to say about Flint's Pond, which is bigger and has more fish, has to do with the fact that it was named for the farmer whose land was next to the pond. Thoreau questions the right of a man who does not see, love, protect, or thank God for a pond to name it after himself. In his estimation the pond would be better named for its fish or flowers. Of Goose Pond and Fair-Haven he has nothing to say. Of White Pond he says mostly that it is like Walden in its color and stony shore. He calls White and Walden ponds "crystals" on the surface of the earth, and says that if they were hardened and small enough to be picked up, they would be carried off, for sure, to crown the heads of emperors.

10. BAKER FARM

Thoreau's ramblings take him past the neighboring
ponds, to pine groves, to cedar woods, to swamps—
all places of beauty that can make the beholder forget
his home. The way others might visit certain people,
Thoreau visits certain trees, be they in some pasture,
wood, swamp, or on a hilltop. He calls them
"shrines." The image of sacred places and holiness
carriers over into the next paragraph, in which Thoreau describes (although with no special reverence)
first standing at one end of a rainbow in a lake of
rainbow light, and then his awareness of a halo of
light surrounding his shadow as he walked.

The train of thought returns to Thoreau's wander-
ings away from Walden Pond. One afternoon he goes
fishing at Fair-Haven. His path takes him through a
meadow that is part of the Baker Farm. As he walks, it
begins to rain and he ends up standing under a tree
for half an hour. He no sooner makes his first cast into
the water when the storm breaks out all over again.
This time Thoreau runs for shelter to a nearby hut that
had been empty for a long while. As it turns out the
hut isn't empty at all, but is now the home of one John
Field, his wife, and their children. Field is an Irishman
who has come to America in search of opportunity
and a better life. He works hard for a neighboring
farmer for very low wages. He is one of those on a
treadmill. It begins with eating—tea, coffee, butter,
milk, and beef—which leads to having to work hard
to pay for them, which leads to having to eat again
after such hard work. Thoreau says, "He was discontented and wasted his life into the bargain."

NOTE: Thoreau is often criticized for his attitudes toward immigrants, especially the Irish who were in the Concord area in great numbers to work on the railroad. His portrait of John Field in this chapter is typical of his attitude.

Thoreau seizes this opportunity to profess to John Field and his wife his own theories of "economy." He tries to help the Fields with the benefit of his own experience. You hear again many of the theories you heard in the first chapter of the book, of housing and clothing and eating and working. And you hear in Thoreau's voice the confidence of a man who has lived his own philosophy and seen it work. He speaks as an American to this Irish immigrant and encourages him to abandon his "old country mode in this primitive new country," adding,

> . . . the only true America is that country where you are at liberty to pursue such a mode of life as may enable you to do without these [tea, coffee, and meat every day], and where the state does not endeavor to compel you to sustain the slavery and war and other superfluous expenses which directly or indirectly result from the use of such things.

John Field and his wife do not seem to understand Thoreau's words, or, at least, how to apply his words to their own plight.

When the rain ends Thoreau leaves the Fields, pausing first for a drink of their water, which turns out to be muddy and warm. You cannot help but compare the muddy water of the Fields' life with the pure, fresh, cold water of Walden Pond. In the water alone we see the difference in the quality of the two ways of life.

The wildness and energy with which Thoreau bounds away from the hut are of the sort you might expect from a man escaping a terrible fate. And a terrible fate it is, that most people accept "through want of enterprise and faith." Thoreau's spirit says, Go far and wide, seek adventures, enjoy the land, while other men come home from the next field, "their shadows, morning and evening, reach farther than their daily steps."

11. HIGHER LAWS

A woodchuck crosses Thoreau's path as he comes home after fishing, and the sight of him provokes a response in Thoreau that you would probably never expect. He says he "felt a strange thrill of savage delight, and was strongly tempted to seize and devour him raw; not that I was hungry then, except for that wildness which he represented."

And so Thoreau admits to a conflict that has arisen in his return to a primitive life-style. While he aspires to a life that is on a high spiritual level, he also desires a harmony with a nature that sometimes has a wild side. He senses the savage within himself, and he respects that tendency as much as he respects his tendency to spiritual elevation.

To fishing and hunting, he owes his experience with nature as a boy. He knows that hunters and fishermen spend a great deal of time in a landscape that they would have little reason to know otherwise. In one sense this familiarity makes them a part of nature, and makes them better able to observe her than poets and philosophers who "approach her with expectation." It is the solitary sports of fishing and hunting that, in the United States, take the place of the games played by boys in England.

While at Walden Thoreau sometimes has a craving for fish as a way of achieving a little variety in his diet. He never pities the fishes or the worms he baits them with. He does not hunt while at Walden. He did hunt in the past when studying new and rare birds, until he decided that it was of more value to study their habits than to kill them. Hunting, even in a civilized society, is a phase that the individual passes through, but, "No humane being, past the thoughtless age of boyhood, will wantonly murder any creature which holds its life by the same tenure that he does."

Fishing now makes him uncomfortable. He respects himself less when he does it, although he still has the instinct to do it. He thinks there "is something essentially unclean" about a diet of fish or any flesh, and the uncleanliness is his chief objection to animal food. It certainly is not that he is squeamish, for he claims to have eaten a fried rat with relish when it was necessary. Like many people attempting to achieve a higher mental state, Thoreau avoided beef and coffee and tea, not because they didn't agree with his body, but because they didn't agree with his imagination. And, as he explains, both the body and the imagination sit down at the same table. The human race, he thinks, will stop eating meat as it becomes more civilized. This will happen in the same way that some savage tribes stopped their practice of cannibalism when educated by more advanced cultures. Likewise, "water is the only drink for a wise man." It is a man's appetite, his devotion to his sense, that defiles him.

"Our whole life is startlingly moral. There is never an instant's truce between virtue and vice." For Thoreau, this dilemma is embodied here, in a man, between his animal and his higher state, between what is natural and what is simply wild—"There is never an instant's truce." To most spiritual leaders, control over our senses and our passions is necessary in a quest for divinity. Sensuality in all forms springs from one impulse, one appetite. And so does purity. In what at first glance appears to be a puzzling and uncharacteristic statement, Thoreau remarks, "Nature is hard to be overcome, but she must be overcome." Would you have thought that you would ever hear such a statement from him? And yet Thoreau recognizes that the wildness, the savage aspects of man's instincts, must be overcome if he is to achieve a higher state and a place of harmony in the natural world.

NOTE: The dilemma in this chapter is the dilemma of a Transcendentalist. The Transcendentalists rejected the idea of knowledge through the *senses* in favor of knowledge through the *intellect*. And they believed that in nature a person can find a vehicle for spiritual growth. And yet it was in *nature* that Thoreau found this savage side, this desire for gratification of the senses. "Higher Laws" is his attempt and failure to reconcile these divergent impulses within himself.

---

12. BRUTE NEIGHBORS

The beginning of this chapter is like nothing else in the book. Thoreau first remarks that sometimes he had a fishing companion, and that catching dinner was as much of a social event as eating it. Then the narrative form is abandoned in favor of a dialogue between one character called the Hermit and another called the Poet. The hermit is Thoreau (he refers to himself with this term again later in the book). The poet is the companion who comes to fish with him. The subject of the dialogue is whether or not the hermit will go fishing with the poet or will attempt instead to regain the thread of his meditation and continue it. The conflict that you witnessed in "Higher Laws" is not yet resolved. Unable to retrace his mental steps once he is interrupted, the hermit decides to go fishing.

Thoreau then reverts to the narrative style of the rest of the book, and wonders at the animals he has for neighbors. His house is inhabited by a wild, native mouse that comes out at lunchtime to eat the crumbs, and that runs up Thoreau's sleeve and eats cheese from his hand. Birds, too, share his domestic life at the pond. A phoebe builds a nest in his shed and a robin builds a nest in a pine tree next to his cabin. The remarkable partridge allows her brood to pass by Thoreau's windows. He describes the eyes of the partridge: "An intelligence seems reflected in them. They suggest not merely the purity of infancy, but a wisdom clarified by experience. Such an eye was not born when the bird was, but is coeval with the sky it reflects." Even here—so close to the village—live wild creatures undetected by human eyes: an otter the size of a small boy, the woodcock, turtle doves, the red squirrel. Even the ants—described here in battle in considerable detail and with much excitement—fall under the close scrutiny of Thoreau. He says they fight as if for some principle, like men. And the more you think about it, the more like men they seem.

His animal neighbors are not limited to wild creatures. Dogs and even cats from the village sometimes happen into the woods. Mention of cats reminds Thoreau of a "winged" cat that lived in a farmhouse in Lincoln before he lived at Walden. Making a reference to Pegasus, the winged horse of mythology, he claims that this would have been the kind of cat for him, "for why should not a poet's cat be winged as well as his horse?"

NOTE: At this point in the chapter the poet and the hermit are the same person. Perhaps this is instruction in how to view the dialogue that began the chapter. The two voices can be the two sides of one man.

In autumn his menagerie includes a loon that comes to bathe and molt at Walden. Thoreau describes a great chase on the water in which he is never able to catch the loon, which howls and laughs and is saved at last by a sudden rain that drives Thoreau away. Ducks, too, are there, "but what beside safety they got by sailing in the middle of Walden I do not know, unless they love its water for the same reason that I do."

13. HOUSE-WARMING

"House-warming" has five sections. In the first section it is the beginning of the fall season in the woods of Lincoln. You find Thoreau competing with the red squirrels and the blue jays for chestnuts, storing them for the winter as a substitute for bread. On one occasion he finds a ground-nut, a sort of wild potato that is now all but unknown: "Cultivation has well-nigh exterminated it." For a moment Thoreau fantasizes about the revival of this native tuber and the disappearance of fatted cattle and the crops of grain raised from imported seed.

The woods, with their trees turning quickly to their autumn colors, appear like an art gallery whose manager has rearranged the paintings each day with an eye to color. As the weather cools, thousands of wasps invade the cabin and disappear into the woodwork to hibernate, to escape the winter and cold. Thoreau, too, now acts with that coming season in mind, sitting often on the northeast shore of the pond, warming himself with the "glowing embers" of the summer sun.

In the second section you find him building his chimney, a job that requires studying masonry. Because his bricks were secondhand and covered with old mortar that had to be removed, Thoreau learned more about his materials than he would have otherwise. Walden Pond is represented in this chimney and fireplace—the stones between the bricks and the white sand in the mortar are from the pond's shore. The job is a slow one, and the chimney rises only a few inches each day. Thoreau consoles himself with the thought that "if it proceeded slowly, it was calculated to endure a long time." He is reminded of the structural independence of chimneys, which often can be seen standing long after their houses have burned to the ground. The chimney is to a house what the spirit is to a man. You should keep the image in mind as you read of this man readying himself for winter at Walden Pond.

After the building of the chimney and the shingling of the house, comes the plastering. The plaster makes the house more comfortable against the cold weather, but it is not as beautiful as the rough interior of boards had been. Thoreau remembers Cato's suggestion that a man keep a store of oil and wine in his cellar in expectation of hard times. By comparison, Thoreau has a cellar full of potatoes, peas, rice, molasses, rye, and cornmeal.

The single room of his cabin is small, too small even "to entertain an echo." Thoreau dreams of a larger house, and his description so closely approximates so many of his ideals that we might think he was describing heaven. Hospitality, he says has become the art of keeping people at the greatest distance, and life is lived as far from its symbols as the parlors of homes are from their kitchens.

Toward the end of this section, showing his respect for the difficulties of plastering, Thoreau tells a story of a well-dressed man who has some bad luck when he tries his hand at the art. The section ends with the image of Thoreau christening his hearth.

The first freezing of the pond is the subject of the fourth section. It is this dark and transparent first ice that offers the best view of the bottom of the pond in shallow places. Thoreau describes looking through it as like looking at a picture behind a glass. He goes on to describe at considerable length the action of air bubbles caught in layers of freezing water.

Now winter has set in and Thoreau retreats into his shell and tries to "keep a bright fire both within my house and within my breast." He goes outside to collect dead wood to burn, and he considers the preservation of the forest. While doing this he is reminded of a time when he accidentally set the Concord woods afire while cooking fish. Throughout the ages wood has held a value to man that is even greater than gold. The stumps Thoreau clears from the land warm him twice—once when he splits them and once when he burns them. They give off more heat than any other fuel.

Smoke streaming from his chimney is a sign to other residents of Walden that Thoreau is awake, for which you might also read "alive." When he goes out for several hours, the fire—his cheerful housekeeper—stays behind; the house is never empty. For the sake of economy Thoreau uses a small stove during his second winter. But in no way does it compare with his open fireplace: cooking loses its poetic quality; the stove stinks up the room, takes up a great deal of space, and worst of all, hides the fire. Thoreau feels as if he has lost a friend—the face he always saw in the flames.

14. FORMER INHABITANTS; AND WINTER VISITORS

This is the first of the three chapters set in winter at Walden Pond. It divides into two sections, the first a recollection of people who formerly lived in the woods nearby; the second an accounting of Thoreau's visitors that winter.

In the first sentence Thoreau claims to have "weathered some merry snow-storms, and spent some cheerful winter evenings" at his hearth. At these times even the owl was quiet and did not hoot. But how convincing is he? When he speaks next of having to "conjure up the former occupants of these woods" he sounds rather like an imprisoned man desperate for mental stimulation.

He conjures up three slaves who, within the memory of some in Concord, lived in the woods near the road to Lincoln: Cato Ingraham, who lost his land to a speculator and whose cellar hole is now filled with sumac and goldenrod; Zilpha, a woman who sang in a loud and shrill voice as she spun linen, and whose house was set on fire by English soldiers during the war of 1812; and Brister Freeman who tended apple trees, and his wife who told fortunes. The land still shows the signs of the Stratton family. Nearer to town, the well is all that's left of Breed's house after it was burned down by mischievous boys. Another well and some lilac bushes are all that remain of people named Nutting and Le Grosse.

Toward Lincoln was a potter named Wyman and, closer in time, an Irishman named Hugh Quoil, a ditcher. All that remains of these homes are dents in the earth, covered wells, and lilacs blooming next to where the doorways stood.

NOTE: In his catalogue Thoreau mentions many people, but has little to say about any of them. He speaks with less enthusiasm about each of these human beings than he did of the partridges in the chapter "Brute Neighbors." He exclaims, "Alas! how little does the memory of these human inhabitants enhance the beauty of the landscape!"

You feel the degree to which Thoreau feels trapped by winter when he speaks in the beginning of the second section of the routine to which winter reduced him. You watch him following his own tracks through the snow, taking exactly the same number of steps of exactly the same length coming and going between his house and the road. He walks for miles in any weather to visit a beech tree or a yellow birch, and spends an entire afternoon watching an owl doze on a branch.

His list of winter visitors is short. It includes a farmer who comes to talk, and a poet who makes the house ring with laughter. It also includes one of "the last of the philosophers," a man who so enhanced the beauty of the landscape that "it seemed the heavens and the earth had met together." Together the hermit and the philosopher whittle "shingles of thought" or wade so "reverently" that "the fishes of thought were not scared from the stream." At last, and in the company of the philosopher, Thoreau's spirit is lifted and rises above winter. It may come as a surprise to you that in this season it is human society, not the past or nature, that is Thoreau's salvation.

15. WINTER ANIMALS

From the frozen ponds Thoreau has a view of familiar landscapes that he has never seen before. He also has new and more direct routes to many places. Walden was usually bare of snow. When it was frozen it was like a yard that he could use only in winter, which was when those in the village could not use their yards.

NOTE: When you read this chapter, you will be reminded of an earlier chapter, "Sounds." Here Thoreau describes the sounds of his winter days and nights, beginning with the familiar hooting owl, the goose, and the cat owl. In this season even the earth makes sounds, what Thoreau calls the "whooping of the ice in the pond . . . as if it were restless," and the cracking of the ground by frost. In this passage you can sense Thoreau's restlessness as well.

Foxes bark as they travel over the snow hunting partridge. The red squirrel runs up and down the sides of the house and over the roof. Animals come to the door of the cabin for the half-bushel of ears of corn Thoreau dumps there: rabbits; the red squirrel, whose motions "imply spectators as much as those of a dancing girl," and who drags away an ear larger than itself "like a tiger with a buffalo"; the blue jays with their discordant screams; flocks of chickadees; and sparrows who light on his shoulder.

Hounds pass by hunting with or without men. Thoreau relates a story of a pack of hounds hunting alone who chase a fox all day, and finally chase it to a hunter sitting in the woods. The hunter kills the fox and the hounds are surprised when they catch up with the fox at last and find him dead. At one time bears were hunted on the Fair Haven Ledges, where a moose has been seen, as well. In the pages of an old diary that belonged to a trader Thoreau finds records of the trading of the skins of grey fox, wild-cat, and deer, none of which inhabits the woods in his day.

Mice thin out the pitch pines around the cabin by gnawing the bark around the base. Hares come to the door to nibble potato parings, and Thoreau cannot imagine a country without rabbits and partridges. They seem to him to be not wild creatures at all, only natural ones. But you hear no ecstasy in his voice when he describes them, and he tells you nothing of a link with the spiritual. Thoreau, it seems, is truly under the spell of winter.

16. THE POND IN WINTER

The first of this chapter's three sections begins with a troubled and frustrated Thoreau finding peace in nature:

> After a still winter night I awoke with the impression that some question had been put to me, which I had been endeavoring in vain to answer in my sleep, as what—how—when—where? But there was dawning Nature, in whom all creatures live, looking in at my broad windows with serene

> and satisfied face, and no question on *her* lips. I
> awoke to an answered question, to Nature and
> daylight.

While he is in this frame of mind the slope of his hill
and even the snow seem to urge him forward, and
you meet a renewed sense of energy in the man.

As you might expect, "The Pond in Winter" is
closely related to the chapter "The Ponds." In it you
see many of the same sights in the light of a different
season. When in the morning Thoreau goes to the
pond for water you hear echoes of his earlier descriptions of Walden. He remarks that the "surface of the
pond, which was so sensitive to every breath, and
reflected every light and shadow, becomes solid to the
depth of a foot or a foot and a half . . . it closes its
eyelids and becomes dormant for three months or
more. This is the same lake that in summer was
described as the "earth's eye." The images of vision
continue when he says that in cutting through the ice
he gained "a window" at his feet. He reminds you, as
he stands on the ice, that, "Heaven is under our feet
as well as over our heads."

He mentions the ice fishermen—rough men who
have done more than they can even talk about. He
sees nature carried out in them, an entire food chain,
link by link: "The perch swallows the grub-worm, the
pickerel swallows the perch, and the fisherman swallows the pickerel; and so all the chinks in the scale of
being are filled." He marvels again at Walden's pickerel, fish he has never seen in any market. When they
are caught, they die. "Easily, with a few convulsive
quirks, they give up their watery ghosts, like a mortal
translated before his time to the thin air of heaven."

In the second section Thoreau sounds Walden
Pond for its bottom, disproving theories that it is bot-
tomless. It is precisely 107 feet at its greatest depth.

> This is a remarkable depth for so small an area; yet
> not an inch of it can be spared by the imagination.
> What if all ponds were shallow? Would it not react
> on the minds of men? I am thankful that this pond
> was made deep and pure for a symbol. While men
> believe in the infinite some ponds will be thought
> to be bottomless.

This passage takes on added dimension since you have seen that he often uses the pond as a metaphor for his own soul or spirit.

Through his surveying Thoreau is able to discover the shape of the bottom of the pond. He finds it is quite regular, and without any of the holes that are thought to trouble the bottoms of similar ponds. In the course of his figuring he notices that where the line showing its longest part crosses the line showing its widest part, is where it happens to be deepest. Likewise it may be with a man—that if we know his shores and his nearby country we may "infer his depth and concealed bottom."

In the third section you meet the ice cutters, a merry race: hundreds of happy men who come each day to remove the skin from Walden in the middle of winter. In a good day they say they can cut out a thousand tons. The blocks of ice piled high look to Thoreau like the "abode of Winter." A heap of ten thousand tons that was left in the winter of 1846–1847 was not quite melted by September of 1848. The pond recovered most of what it lost.

"Like the water, the Walden ice, seen near at hand, has a green tint, but at a distance is beautifully blue," says Thoreau in yet another echo of the chapter "The Ponds." The difference between water and ice is the same as the difference between the affections and the intellect. After a while water becomes putrid. When frozen, it remains sweet forever.

Thoreau's imagination wanders abroad with the ice industry, and he thinks of those in warm climates who will drink at Walden Pond, so to speak, when they receive the shipment from its shores.

NOTE: In the days before refrigeration, the ice industry was big business. Ice was cut from ponds such as Walden and shipped to South America, the Caribbean, and Africa.

To a man who studied Eastern philosophy, this was an attractive image. It was that of the servant of the high priest coming to Walden for his master's water, and of their buckets grating against each other there, in the same well.

It may still be winter, but in the pond Thoreau has found an image of spiritual vitality.

17. SPRING

Thoreau claims that as bodies of water go, Walden is still the best indicator of "the absolute progress of the seasons." He reassures us that the actions of the ice cutters will not cause the pond to break up any earlier than would be natural that year. He describes the melting of the ice in great detail and says that in some ways, and on a small scale, "the phenomena of the year take place every day in a pond." This leads him to draw the larger conclusion that, "The day is an epitome of the year. The night is the winter, the morning and evening are the spring and fall, and the noon is the summer." In this passage you hear an echo of a line from an earlier chapter, "Where I Lived, and What I Lived For," in which he says that morning is "the most memorable season of the day."

Being able to watch spring unfold was one of the main attractions of living in the woods, and as the second section of this chapter begins, Thoreau is alert to spring's first signs—the note of a bird, the lengthening day. He describes his favorite springtime phenomenon, the thawing of sand and clay on the deep sides of an embankment near the railroad tracks. The melting sand and clay flow down the sides of the bank in a formation that reminds him of lava, "of coral, of leopards' paws or birds' feet, of brains or lungs or bowels, and excrements of all kinds. It is a truly *grotesque* vegetation," which finally takes the shapes of leaves. You may wonder why Thoreau finds this repulsive image so attractive. One reason may be that it shows us an image of rebirth from a state of decay. This is spring, says Thoreau, and it "precedes the green and flowery spring, as mythology precedes regular poetry."

In the third section, as the ground thaws and the signs of spring mingle with the remnants of winter, you hear the first sparrow, the bluebird, the song sparrow, and a red-wing. You see the sun return, and then the grass, which like human life dies back only to the root and grows again toward eternity.

After all the chapters of winter, Walden is melting. "Walden was dead and is alive again," says Thoreau, who is beside himself with rejoicing at this "memorable crisis." The pond seems to reflect the calm and hope of a summer sky already, even though there is no such evening overhead. Thoreau listens to a robin's song and expresses his joy at hearing it with this exaggeration: it was "the first I had heard for many a thousand years . . . whose note I shall not forget for many a thousand more."

Thoreau says that "every season seems best to us in
its turn," but you know him better than this by now.
You have heard his voice in summer, fall, winter, and
spring, and you know that for him, spring is best.

As happier thoughts occur to him, his prospects
brighten. It is much the same process as the grass
growing greener in a gentle rain. In every image Thoreau rejoices at the season, like a man liberated. This is
what he needed all along:

> We need the tonic of wildness. . . . At the same
> time that we are earnest to explore and learn all
> things, we require that all things be mysterious
> and unexplorable that land and sea be infinitely
> wild, unsurveyed, and unfathomed by us because
> unfathomable. We can never have enough of
> nature. . . . We need to witness our own limits
> transgressed, and some life pasturing freely where
> we never wander.

The chapter ends abruptly, with two sentences that
announce the end of Thoreau's life in the woods. He
left Walden on September 6, 1847.

18. CONCLUSION

The conclusion of Walden begins with this sentence: "To the sick the doctors wisely recommend a
change of air and scenery." For the ailing spirit Thoreau has recommendations of his own. It is not necessary to travel abroad. Thoreau uses references to
explorers, routes of travel and trade, and far-off lands
to tell you the folly of any search that begins outside
yourself: "be a Columbus to whole new continents
and worlds within you, opening new channels, not of
trade, but of thought." This is what his life at Walden
was all about.

He explains why he left:

> I left the woods for as good a reason as I went
> there. Perhaps it seemed to me that I had several
> more lives to live, and could not spare any more
> time for that one. . . . I learned this, at least, by my
> experiment: that if one advances confidently in the
> direction of his dreams, and endeavors to live the
> life which he has imagined, he will meet with a
> success unexpected in common hours. . . . If you
> have built castles in the air, your work need not be
> lost; that is where they should be. Now put the
> foundations under them.

In one paragraph after another Thoreau speaks
"like a man in a waking moment, to men in their waking moments." You remember that in his vocabulary,
awake is another word for "alive." He says that in trying to make you understand, in trying to lay a foundation for his truths, he cannot exaggerate enough. In
an inspirational voice, and in what reads at times like
an inspired sermon, he urges you to be what you can.
Ignore claims that people of modern times are "intellectual dwarfs compared with the ancients," he
insists. "A living dog is better than a dead lion."

And here he utters one of his most famous remarks,
his support of each person growing at his own rate.
"If a man does not keep pace with his companions,
perhaps it is because he hears a different drummer.
Let him step to the music which he hears, however
measured or far away."

In one quotable and quoted line after another, he
urges a singlemindedness of purpose, a life filled with
resolution and lived according to the truth. Meet life
and live it, however mean it is; "do not trouble yourself much to get new things . . . things do not change;
we change." He urges humility which, like darkness,
makes it possible to see the heavenly lights of stars.

He warns against a desire for great sums of money—more than enough money buys only more than enough. Words such as *joy* and *sorrow* belong in the vocabulary of your life, not merely in the vocabulary of prayer books.

As the chapter draws to a close Thoreau tells a story of a beautiful insect that came out of a table made of apple-wood. The egg from which the insect hatched had been laid in the living tree years before the tree was made into a table. The table itself had stood in a farmer's kitchen for sixty years when, stimulated by the warmth of an urn put on the table, the dormant insect began to gnaw its way out of the wood.

In each of us there may be such an egg, the beginning of a beautiful life, which so far has been buried under layers of dry, wooden, and dead life which is society. That beginning may some day at last gnaw its way out of some trivial furniture to enjoy a life, with wings.

In the final paragraph of the book Thoreau admits that not everyone will understand him, not everyone who reads his words will take them to heart. He leaves you with an image that is at once a warning and an expression of hope: "The light which puts out our eyes is darkness to us. Only that day dawns to which we are awake. There is more day to dawn. The sun is but a morning star."

A STEP BEYOND

Tests and Answers

TESTS

Test 1

1. For Thoreau the Walden adventure was _____ essentially
   A. an escape from civilized society
   B. a demonstration of his independent spirit
   C. an attempt to find the height and depth of his inner self

2. According to Thoreau, an important in- _____ gredient in reaching a union with nature is
   A. purification of the channels of perception
   B. maintenance of a strict regimen
   C. elimination of all but the most basic social contacts

3. Thoreau regarded the Puritan work ethic as _____
   A. ennobling man's nature
   B. necessary to existence
   C. debasing man's higher nature

4. For Thoreau the most memorable season of _____ the day is
   A. the awakening hour
   B. the tranquil night
   C. dependent on an individual's mood

5. The time Thoreau actually spent at Walden _____
   was about
   A. one year
   B. two years
   C. three years

6. The imagery of the reptile shedding its skin is _____
   compared to
   A. spring
   B. summer
   C. autumn

7. "The mass of men lead lives of quiet _____
   desperation" means that
   A. men are generally ill suited to their work
      but suffer in silence
   B. work usually prevents men from realizing
      their inner potential
   C. happiness is God-given rather than
      attained by human effort

8. Thoreau calculates the cost of his cabin was _____
   A. $28
   B. $165
   C. $247

9. Thoreau suggests he liked to entertain guests _____
   in
   A. his house
   B. his "withdrawing room . . . behind my
      house"
   C. on the shore of the pond

10. At Walden Thoreau is visited by _____
    A. women and young children from town
    B. runaway slaves
    C. both A and B

11. What is the experiment that is conducted in *Walden*, why is it conducted, and does it succeed?

12. Discuss Walden Pond as the principal symbol in the book. What does it symbolize and how does its role change during the course of the book?

13. Define slavery as seen in *Walden*.

14. What relation does the structure of the book have to the natural world?

15. In what ways does Thoreau's experiment *depend* on civilization?

Test 2

1. Thoreau's pleasure in the bean-field he _____
   harvested is that
   A. it has attached him to the earth, increasing his kinship with nature
   B. he has learned the lost art of "true husbandry," which concentrates on studied cultivation rather than material gain
   C. its profits afforded him the means to complete his stay at Walden

2. On one of his trips to the village, Thoreau _____
   A. is jailed for aiding a runaway slave
   B. is jailed for refusing to pay a tax
   C. loses his way in the deep woods

3. In speaking of John Field at Baker Farm, _____
   Thoreau laments that
   A. they were unsuccessful in their fishing expedition
   B. despite their hard work life has brought the Fields little
   C. men's shadows morning and evening reach farther than their daily steps

4. Thoreau believes "the animal in us" _____
   A. can be rooted out by abstinence from meat and strong drink
   B. must be controlled in the unending struggle between good and evil
   C. gives us the strength to become all that nature has intended

5. The chapter "Brute Neighbors" discourses _____
on
   A. the ferocious battle between the black and
   the red ants
   B. the dehumanizing spectacle of the
   drunkards in the village
   C. drudgery and savagery of life among the
   common village folk

6. In general, winter _____
   A. brings Thoreau closer to his purpose in
   Walden because it forces him to
   "internalize" his life
   B. brings him equal though different
   opportunities, compared to other seasons,
   to realize his goal
   C. leaves him less contented in his desire to be
   one with nature

7. The idea of people from Charleston or New _____
Orleans drinking at his well refers to the
   A. water obtained from the ice chopped from
   the pond
   B. ideas that Thoreau lives by finding their
   way to other cities
   C. fact that he has entertained visitors from
   many places

8. The parable of the Indian artist who made a _____
perfect staff illustrates
   A. why Thoreau left Walden
   B. that some men march to a different
   drummer
   C. that we need not tolerate dullness when
   there is constant novelty in the world

9. To attain self-emancipation Thoreau preached _____
   A. self-imposed poverty
   B. simplification
   C. both A and B

10. Thoreau finds the Canadian woodchopper _____
    to
    A. have a slumbering mind
    B. be a kindred spirit who has learned to commune with nature
    C. be unhappy with the world

11. If it had been possible for Thoreau to return completely to primitive life, would he have done so? What is the evidence? Explain.

12. Discuss some of the problems that are *not* resolved in *Walden*.

13. Discuss the dynamic of *Walden*, its movement from the single fact to the universal truth. Give examples of both thoughts and metaphors in which this is shown.

14. Discuss Thoreau's use of time in *Walden*.

15. Discuss the bean-field in *Walden*.

ANSWERS

Test 1

1. C **2.** A **3.** C **4.** A **5.** B **6.** A
7. B **8.** A **9.** B **10.** C

11. In answering this question you should first present the facts: Thoreau built his own house and lived alone at Walden for two years doing only as much work as was necessary to meet his expenses. Review some of the principles expressed in the first chapter, "Economy," in terms of his life-style while at Walden Pond. Then present the philosophy behind the facts: Thoreau's wish to live "as deliberately as Nature," and to make himself rich by making his wants few. For this part of the essay, consult Chapter 2, "Where I Lived, and What I Lived For."

In trying to decide whether it was a success or a failure, think about the rest of the book, the "Conclusion" in particular. There Thoreau tells you what the experiment achieved. You might wish to consider, too, that the "experiment" did not last forever.

12. Discuss this symbol from a number of angles. Go into the many times that bathing in the pond is a symbol of baptism and renewal ("Where I Lived, and What I Lived For" and "The Village"). Discuss the images of the pond as an organ of vision ("Where I Lived, and What I Lived For," "The Ponds," and "The Pond in Winter") as well as the images of connection between heaven and earth that are found in these chapters. Keep in mind the cycle that the pond follows during the year, and compare this to the phases that Thoreau himself goes through.

13. *Walden* was written before the outbreak of the Civil War in the United States, and slavery was very much an issue at the time. Thoreau mentions in *Walden* (in "Visitors") that one of his visitors was a runaway slave, whom he helped. Refer to the chapter "Economy" in which Thoreau portrays men as slaves to the necessities of life as they earn money to pay their rent and buy food. Mention the image in that chapter of the wealthy in their gold and silver fetters. And discuss his remarks, also in this chapter, about the "keen and subtle masters that enslave both North and South," and about Negro slavery being a foreign form of servitude in comparison.

14. Both the actual experiment and the book begin in the spring, a time of rebirth and renewal on earth. Thoreau collapses his stay of two years into one for the purposes of telling the story. Notice how the book makes a complete cycle from one spring to another, and the man does too. Discuss the symbolism involved in this cyclical structuring (which involves everything from the pond to the house).

15. This question should be answered on two levels. The first is practical. Thoreau used tools, information, and techniques that are the products of civilization in the building of his house and the surveying of the area of Walden Pond (see "The Pond in Winter"). His path to town is the railroad track.

The second level is spiritual. Thoreau, in his search for elevation, drew on the wisdom of the past, as all Transcendentalists would. His mental state was influenced by Eastern mysticism and the classics, what he calls in "Reading" the "trophies of civilization."

Test 2

1. A **2.** B **3.** C **4.** B **5.** A **6.** C
7. A **8.** B **9.** C **10.** A

11. Much of the evidence you need to answer this question will come from the chapter "Visitors" in which Thoreau describes a Canadian woodchopper who was often in the forest. Thoreau discusses this man in great detail, gives you a pretty good idea of how he feels about a human being who is so "natural." You might also want to consider the chapter "Former Inhabitants; and Winter Visitors," and who it is who finally lightens up Thoreau's winter, as well as the chapters "Reading" and "Higher Laws."

12. The parts of the book that will be most useful in answering this question are the end of Chapter 11, "Higher Laws," and the beginning of Chapter 12, "Brute Neighbors." The conflict between the desire for harmony with the natural world and the wildness and sensuality that exist *in* that world is well expressed here. You might want to consider the Transcendentalist position on the senses when explaining the statement that nature must be overcome.

13. It would be helpful here to follow the image of the sun in the book, from the remark that Thoreau has his own sun, moon, and stars, to the one about the same sun illuminating his bean-field as illuminates another world. Discuss this as a movement from a consideration of the individual to a consideration of society.

14. In an essay on this topic you could consider time from a number of angles. It could be broken down into different units of time and discussed accordingly. Thoreau discusses morning as the best season of the day (in "Where I Lived, and What I Lived For") and later amplifies that image in a discussion of all parts of the day ("Spring"). He has much to say about the seasons, and the structure of the book should also be a factor in your discussion. And throughout the book (especially in "Economy" and "Where I Lived, and What I Lived For") he mentions time as something that must not be wasted.

15.   Any discussion of the bean-field should be twofold. In "Economy" Thoreau introduces the bean-field as a factor in his system of economy, a means of generating income. He supplies you with all the figures on its profits.

In "The Bean-Field" it takes on another importance—that of a link between what is wild in nature and what is cultivated. As a symbol it is important for that reason. Be sure to review this chapter before answering the question.

Term Paper Ideas

1. For what is the railroad a symbol in *Walden?*

2. How does Thoreau use the image of the sun?

3. What part does the philosopher, as seen by Thoreau, play in society?

4. What does Thoreau mean by the word *awake?*

5. In what ways does Thoreau write about what we now call ecology?

6. In what ways does Thoreau use references to myth in *Walden?*

7. Does Thoreau emerge as a naturalist or as a poet in the book?

8. Is Walden Pond improved by Thoreau's stay there?

9. Discuss the influence that Thoreau had on the landscape.

10. Is life at Walden Pond lonely for Thoreau? Explain.

11. What influence did the Transcendental movement have on Thoreau?

12. What are the implications to society of Thoreau's experiment?

13. Discuss Thoreau's explanation of "doubleness."

14. Is Thoreau a religious man? Explain.

15. What effect does keeping a journal have on Thoreau's writing style?

16. In what ways is *Walden* like great books as Thoreau described them?

17. Describe the imagery of the day in the book.

18. Discuss the imagery of vision in the book.

19. In what ways does Walden Pond differ in winter from other times of the year?

20. What, to Thoreau, is the cost of a thing?

21. Discuss Thoreau's attitude toward wasting time.

22. Where in Walden do we find the beginnings of thoughts expressed more fully in *Civil Disobedience?*

23. Give examples of times when civilization triumphs over wildness in *Walden.*

24. Give examples of times when human companionship is preferable to solitude.

25. Discuss the frequent image of rising or climbing in *Walden.*

26. How does Thoreau use symbols of decay in the book?

27. Discuss how Thoreau saw himself in relation to the rest of the world.

28. It has been said that Thoreau was at times so intent on discovering the bird behind the bird that he neglected to see the bird itself. Discuss.

29. What was Thoreau's opinion of explorers and exploration?

30. How is the chimney used as a symbol in *Walden?*

31. In what very important way did Thoreau differ from Emerson as a philosopher?

32. In what way are the ants like men?

33. Discuss Thoreau's attitude toward hunting and fishing.

34. Discuss Thoreau's diet and his attitudes toward food.

35. What is the function of the news in our society?

Further Reading

CRITICAL WORKS

Derleth, August. *Concord Rebel: A Life of Henry D. Thoreau.* Philadelphia: Chilton, 1962. A biography for young readers.

Harding, Walter. *The Days of Henry Thoreau.* New York: Alfred A. Knopf, 1965. A biography of Thoreau by a notable scholar, and the editor of his correspondence.

————. ed. *The Thoreau Centennial.* Yellow Springs, Ohio: Antioch Press, 1965. A collection of essays about the author compiled some one hundred years after his death.

————. *A Thoreau Handbook.* New York: New York University Press, 1959. Essays about the life and work of Thoreau, and a complete guide to research on this topic.

————. *Thoreau: A Century of Criticism.* Dallas: Southern Methodist University Press, 1954. A selection of criticism written in the one hundred years since the publication of *Walden.*

————. *Thoreau: Man of Concord.* New York: Holt, Rinehart and Winston, 1960. An anthology of profiles of the author by those who knew him.

Krutch, Joseph Wood. *Henry David Thoreau.* New York: William Sloane, 1948. A biography.

Lane, Luriat, Jr., ed. *Approaches to Walden.* San Francisco: Wadsworth, 1961. A comprehensive introduction to the study of *Walden,* including a bibliography, criticism, essays, and information about the author.

Matthiessen, F. O. *The American Renaissance: Art and Expression in the Age of Emerson and Whitman.* New York: Oxford University Press, 1948. A very readable critical approach to influences in literature in Thoreau's time and among writers he admired. It includes the often quoted essay, "*Walden:* Craftsmanship vs. Technique."

Paul, Sherman, ed. *Thoreau: A Collection of Critical Essays*. Englewood Cliffs, N.J.: Prentice-Hall, 1962. A collection of some of the more well-known essays by critics of our time.

AUTHOR'S OTHER WORKS

Walden is not Thoreau's only famous work, although it may be the one people think of most often in connection with his name. *Civil Disobedience* (1849) has had great influence the world over as a political tract, and to some people it is better known than *Walden* itself. A list of Thoreau's other works and their dates of publication follows.

A Week on the Concord and Merrimack Rivers, 1849

The Maine Woods, 1864

Cape Cod, 1865

Letters to Various Persons, 1865

A Yankee in Canada, 1866

Journals (14 volumes), 1906

Collected Poems of Henry David Thoreau, 1943

The Correspondence of Henry David Thoreau, 1958

Glossary

Agrarian society A society based on farming in which division of land and land reforms reflects the interests and economic status of the farmer.

Antaeus In Greek mythology, a son of Poseidon and Ge (the Earth); a wrestler who derived his strength from touching the earth (his mother) and who was killed when Hercules lifted him off the ground.

Astrology A belief that a person's destiny is influenced by the arrangement of planets and stars.

Astronomy The science of celestial bodies, and the laws that govern their motions.

Bramin (also Brahmin or Brahman) The highest of the four Hindu castes or social classes.

Cato Marcus Porcius Cato, 234–149 B.C., a Roman statesman who is known for his writings about agriculture.

Confucius A Chinese philosopher born in the middle of the 6th century B.C. He was a teacher of morality who believed in the power of example. He was one of Thoreau's favorite authors.

Cultivate To prepare for growing of crops; to till; to improve; to refine.

Divine Relating to the deity or gods; godlike.

Division of labor A term referring to modern manufacturing in which each person does only a part of the process (for the sake of efficiency) and depends on the cooperation of others.

Economy The frugal use of resources or the management of expenses; in Thoreau's vocabulary, the management and organization of one's life.

Epitome Embodiment.

Hercules A hero of classical mythology known for his great strength.

Hindu An inhabitant of India; one who practices the Indian religion of Hinduism.

Homer Greek poet, author of the epic poems *The Iliad* and *The Odyssey*.

Husbandry The raising or management of plants and animals; farming.

Iliad The epic poem by Homer about the fall of Troy.

Industrial Revolution The name given to the change from an agricultural to an industrial society that took place in the late 1800s and the early part of the 1900s.

Manual labor Literally, work done with the hands, but also any work that requires physical activity.

Nature The external world in its original state, and the controlling force in the universe.

Olympus In classical mythology, the mountain on which the gods lived.

Philanthropy Humanitarianism; good will toward mankind.

Philosopher One who develops theories about the nature of truth.

Philosophy A search for wisdom and truth through reasoning rather than through observation of facts; belief.

Railroad The Fitchburg-Boston line, built by Irish immigrants, which connected Concord with Boston and passed close to the shore of Walden Pond.

Society In *Walden* this most often means the company of others, but it also means a social group or community.

Transcendentalism A philosophy that stresses the spiritual and the intellectual rather than the material and the sensual.

Vedas Ancient Hindu scriptures.

The Critics

On Thoreau's Development

It [*Walden*] is a recapitulation of Thoreau's development (and the artistic reason he put the experience of
two years into one)—a development from the sensu-
ous, active, external (unconscious *and* out-of-doors)
summer of life, through the stages of autumnal consciousness and the withdrawal inward to the self-
reflection of winter, to the promise of ecstatic rebirth in
the spring.

Sherman Paul, "Resolution at Walden," in
Thoreau, *1962*

Putting Theory Into Practice

But if Thoreau's retirement was rather a gesture than
an adventure, it was also what gestures at their most
striking must become—namely, a symbol, and to his
often very downright mind the importance of the symbol lay in part in the fact that it involved certain acts
which, however unspectacular, were nevertheless visible and concrete attempts to put into some sort of actual
practice theories which could not honorably be allowed
to remain merely theories. Emerson might talk about
plain living and about breaking with convention, but
there was nothing in his outward way of life capable of
shocking the most conventional. He did not *do* anything. He did not take even a first step. He was, as a
matter of fact, always to hold himself aloof from the
experiments in which other Transcendentalists, even
finally Hawthorne, were to become involved in. Thoreau wanted to begin to live some special kind of life,
not merely to think about one.

Joseph Wood Krutch, Henry David
Thoreau, *1948*

On Thoreau's Style

Thoreau was perhaps more precise about his own
style and more preoccupied generally with literary craft
than any American writer except Henry James. He

rewrote endlessly, not only, like James, for greater precision, but unlike James, for greater simplicity. "Simplify, Simplify, Simplify," he gave as the three cardinal principles of both life and art. Emerson had said of Montaigne: "Cut these words and they would bleed" and Thoreau's is perhaps the only American style in his century of which this is true. Criticizing De Quincey, he stated his own prose aesthetic, "the *art* of writing," demanding sentences that are concentrated and nutty, that suggest far more than they say, that are kinked and knotted into something hard and significant, to be swallowed like a diamond without digesting.

> Stanley Edgar Hyman, "Henry Thoreau
> in Our Time," 1963

It was Thoreau's conviction that by reducing life to its primitive conditions, he had come to the roots from which healthy art must flower. . . . The light touch of his detachment allows the comparison of his small things with great, and throughout the book enables him to possess the universe at home.

> F. O. Matthiessen, "Walden:
> Craftsmanship vs. Technique," 1948

Was Thoreau a Sentimentalist?

To seek to be natural implies a consciousness that forbids all naturalness forever. It is as easy—and no easier—to be natural in a *salon* as in a swamp, if one does not aim at it, for what we call unnaturalness always has its spring in a man's thinking too much about himself. . . . To a man of wholesome constitution the wilderness is well enough for a mood or a vacation, but not for the habit of life. Those who have most loudly advertised their passion for seclusion and their intimacy with nature . . . have been mostly sentimentalists, unreal men, misanthropes on the spindle side, solacing an uneasy suspicion of themselves by professing contempt for their kind.

> Ralph Waldo Emerson, "Thoreau," 1862

NOTES

NOTES

Sounds

Brute Neighbors

Ponds

Spritiual metaphor
of Thoreau